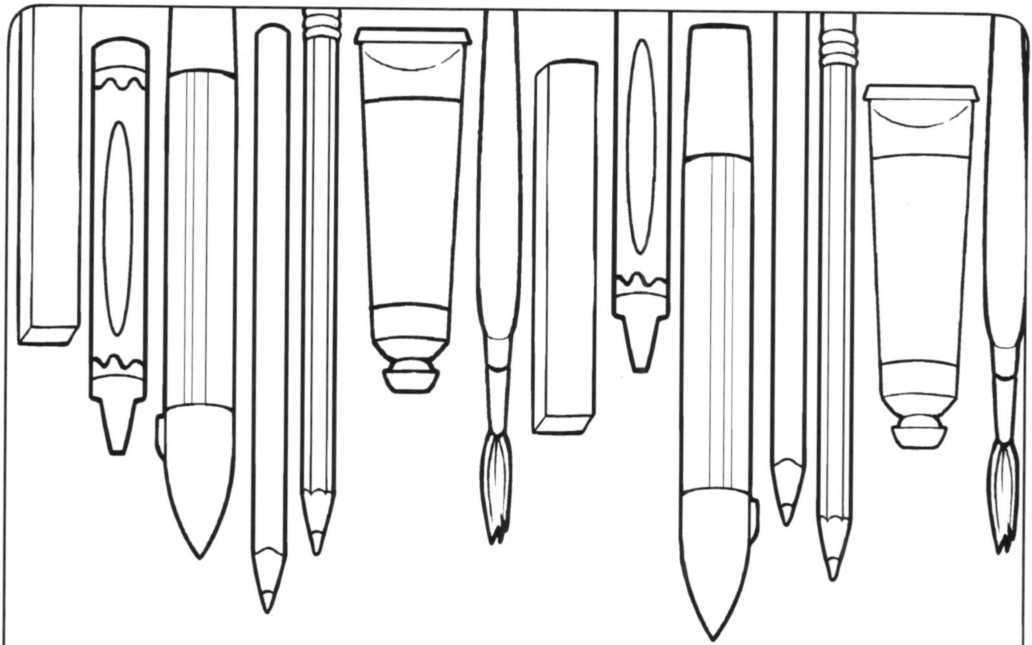

HOW TO USE THIS BOOK

When coloring, I recommend for you to place a thick and/or bleedproof piece of paper behind the page you are working on. This will prevent any color from leaking onto the subsequent pages and also save them from getting any dents or marks. The pages are all single-sided so you can use a variety of mediums freely. Crayons, gel pens, colored pencls, alcohol-based markers, regular markers, and more will work!

Have fun coloring!

-YamPuff

Color Charts: Color Collection Edition

yampuff.deviantart.com
Cover and Book design by Yasmeen Eldahan

ISBN-13: 978-1539013150
ISBN-10: 1539013154

Thank you!

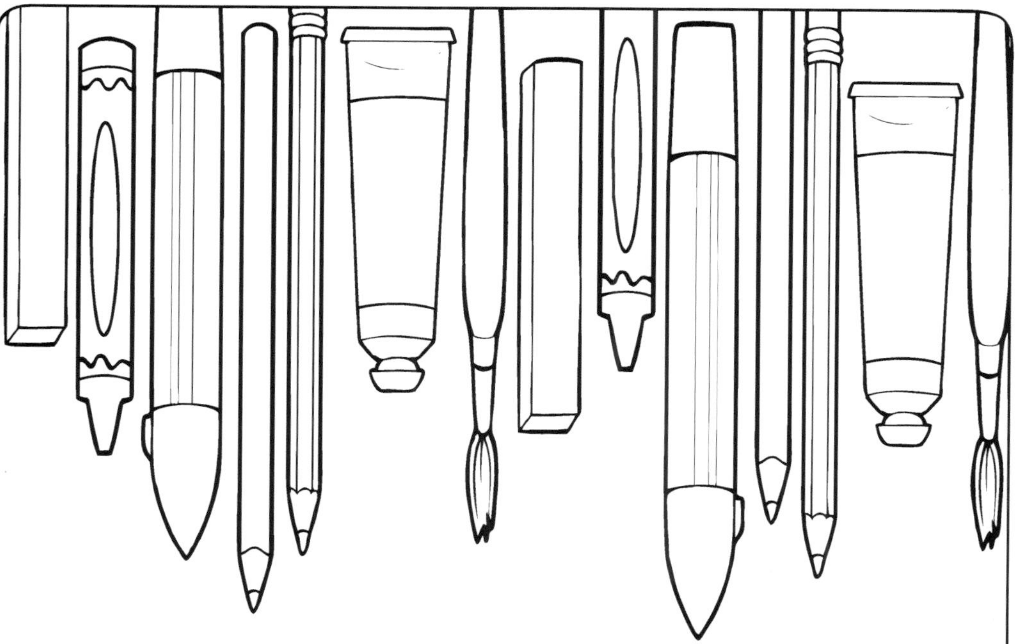

CONNECT WITH ME!

Check out my art, coloring contests, free linearts and more:

- halfbakedyams.tumblr.com/
- facebook.com/YamPuff
- instagram.com/halfbakedyams/
- twitter.com/HalfBakedYams
- pinterest.com/yampuff/
- yampuff.deviantart.com/

Or check out my shops for digital stamps, stickers and other merch:

- etsy.com/shop/YamPuffsStuff
- redbubble.com/people/yampuff/shop
- zazzle.com/yampuff

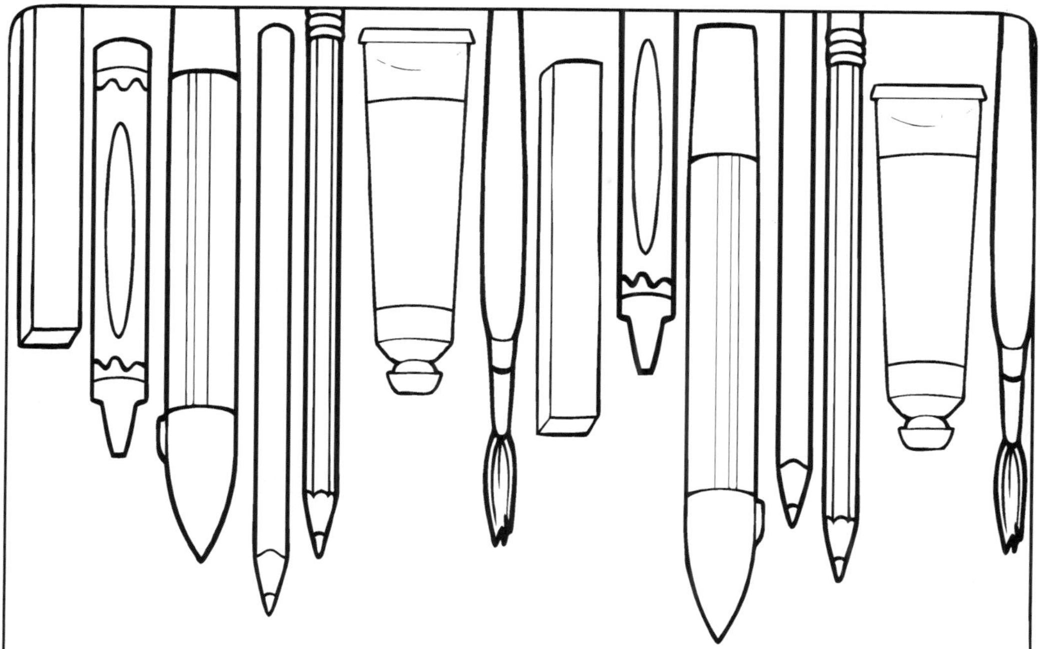

THIS BOOK BELONGS TO:

COLOR CHART ______________________ DATE ______________

COLOR CHART ____________________ **DATE** ____________

COLOR CHART ______________________ **DATE** ______________

COLOR CHART ______________ DATE ______________

COLOR CHART ______________________ DATE ______________

COLOR CHART

DATE

COLOR CHART ____________________ DATE ______________

COLOR CHART ______________________ DATE ______________

COLOR CHART ________________ DATE ________________

COLOR CHART

DATE

COLOR CHART ____________ DATE ____________

COLOR CHART

DATE

COLOR CHART

DATE

COLOR CHART ______________________ **DATE** ____________

COLOR CHART

DATE

COLOR CHART

DATE

COLOR CHART ______ DATE ______

COLOR CHART

DATE

COLOR CHART ____________________ DATE ____________

COLOR CHART ______________________ DATE ____________

COLOR CHART ____________________ **DATE** ____________

COLOR CHART ____________________ **DATE** ____________

COLOR CHART ______________________ **DATE** ______________

COLOR CHART ____________________ DATE ____________

COLOR CHART

DATE

COLOR CHART ____________________ DATE ____________

☐ ________	☐ ________	☐ ________
☐ ________	☐ ________	☐ ________
☐ ________	☐ ________	☐ ________
☐ ________	☐ ________	☐ ________
☐ ________	☐ ________	☐ ________
☐ ________	☐ ________	☐ ________
☐ ________	☐ ________	☐ ________
☐ ________	☐ ________	☐ ________
☐ ________	☐ ________	☐ ________
☐ ________	☐ ________	☐ ________
☐ ________	☐ ________	☐ ________
☐ ________	☐ ________	☐ ________
☐ ________	☐ ________	☐ ________
☐ ________	☐ ________	☐ ________
☐ ________	☐ ________	☐ ________

COLOR CHART ______ DATE ______

COLOR CHART

DATE

COLOR CHART ______________________ DATE ____________

COLOR CHART ______________________ DATE ____________

COLOR CHART ______________ DATE ______________

COLOR CHART ______________________ DATE ______________

COLOR CHART ____________________ DATE ____________

COLOR CHART

DATE

COLOR CHART ______________________ **DATE** ______________

COLOR CHART ______________________ DATE ______________

COLOR CHART ______ DATE ______

COLOR CHART ____________________ DATE ____________

COLOR CHART ____________ DATE ____________

COLOR CHART ______________________ DATE ______________

COLOR CHART ______________________ **DATE** ____________

COLOR CHART ______ DATE ______

COLOR CHART ____________________ DATE ____________

COLOR CHART ______ DATE ______

COLOR CHART ______________ DATE ______________

COLOR CHART ____________________ DATE ____________

COLOR CHART ____________________ DATE ____________

COLOR CHART ______________________ **DATE** ______________

COLOR CHART ______________________ DATE ____________

COLOR CHART ______________________ DATE ____________

Uploading what you've colored? Tag it with
#YAMPUFF
I would love to see (and share) your work!

YamPuff's Stuff

Carousel Dreams

Want to color even more?
Check out my coloring books!

Available on amazon.com

And as digital eBook downloads
@ etsy.com/shop/YamPuffsStuff

73954473R00061

Made in the USA
Lexington, KY
13 December 2017